RETELLING
GENESIS

by Barry Louis Polisar   illustrations by Roni Polisar

Multiple translations were used as source material for these stories including the Artscroll Stone Chumash, the Soncino Chumash, the Etz Hayim and Torah translations from the Jewish Publication Society, and Professor Robert Alter's 1996 translation and commentary on Genesis.

Thanks to my daughter Sierra, who planted the seeds for this book over a decade ago, when she came home with a school assignment to rewrite a well-known story and chose to write about Noah's wife; to Rabbi Jonah Layman for his enduring patience in continuing to answer all my questions, week after week, in a Torah study class where we are encouraged to raise questions and wrestle with the things we read; to Rabbi Bob Saks for his insightful observations and thoughtful suggestions; to Pat Myers for her astute comments as she edited these stories; to Zachary Newman and Susan Valliant for editing and commenting on my early drafts; and to my wife, Roni, who not only repeatedly read and made helpful suggestions on the text, but created the perfect illustrations to accompany them.

INTRODUCTION

The stories in the book of Genesis – known in Hebrew as B'reishit – have helped shape our moral and ethical foundation. Ironically, many of these stories are about troubled people with imperfections, jealousies and flaws. These people may even be called the first dysfunctional family.

Through the ages, religious leaders and commentators have sought to "explain" the personal failings of our patriarchs and matriarchs, while demonizing other characters in the stories.

There is a long tradition of Midrash as part of study – a way to fill in the gaps left in the original narrative, by telling new stories that offer added insights. Some of the stories that were written to help fill in these details actually contradict the text of Genesis.

The stories I tell here may initially seem a bit irreverent, but a careful reading reveals they are consistent with both the theme and spirit of Genesis. Likewise, God is referenced in the masculine form in a few of the early stories, because that is consistent with the ancient writings my characters are responding to.

Instead of making up a new narrative, I tried to imagine the thoughts and emotions of characters whose perspectives have been ignored in the original text. I think their viewpoints serve as a counterpoint to the original stories and, in the spirit of Midrash, perhaps will offer some new insights.

Barry Louis Polisar, 2014

EVE'S SIDE

I am Eve, made not from clay, but from a rib pulled out of Adam's side. Spared from death, we were both cast out of Eden, clothed in skins and God's mercy.

I am "the woman" in the story and often blamed for this apple thing, but believe me, this was no ordinary fruit. This was the fruit from the Tree of Knowledge of Good and Evil. God never told *me* not to eat from it – at least not directly. He told Adam. I wasn't even around yet when that rule was handed down.

I was, after all, the last to be created. After the swarms of living creatures and the fowl that fly above the earth. After the great sea monsters and the winged birds of every kind. After the cattle, the creeping things, and the wild beasts. After the shrubs and grasses.

After Adam.

God created all of these and pronounced them good. He saw that it was Paradise and that it was holy, and then He rested. It was then that God told Adam not to eat from that tree. And only then did He cause Adam to slumber, and I was created.

 "Just touching the fruit of that tree would kill me," I told the serpent. When that didn't happen, it was easy to assume that Adam had made the whole story up. That's the thing about adding extra rules and prohibitions: you build your fence too high and you run the risk that it will fall from its own weight.

So, yes, first I held the fruit, and then I tasted it – and then I offered it to Adam and he ate. If Adam knew we weren't supposed to eat from the tree, why did he taste that fruit so readily and with not one word of protest – and then blame the whole thing on me? "The woman whom *You* gave me, gave it to me," he whined to God, as if it were *His* fault for creating me to begin with.

I tasted the fruit of that tree when the cunning serpent deceived me, and for that, God cursed me with the pangs of childbirth. I have labored against these pains ever since. Only then was I named Eve, the Mother of all.

CAIN'S MARK

My mark is not a stigma, as people think of it nowadays. "He has the mark of Cain," they say, and make it sound like a scar — as if my own humiliation were not stigma enough. We did not know about murder then. Life was still so new.

No, it was meant to be a sign of protection, put there by God Himself after I pleaded with Him. I lived in fear of what others might do to me if they heard what I had done to my own brother. "What others?" you ask. Wasn't it just Adam and Eve and myself then?

How could there be others to hear of my deed? And how then could I go off and dwell in the land of Nod, condemned to wander east of Eden until I could find a wife to bear me a son? Ah, that is a mysterious thing, I admit. As mysterious as the Nephilim giants that are no longer. But it is not for me to answer. I am not my brother's keeper nor the keeper of any answers. I have only questions.

And what of my story? It is a simple one: I, a humble tiller of the soil, killed my own brother, Abel, a shepherd, and now I am condemned to be a restless wanderer. God warned me that evil and bitterness lurked outside the door, crouching low, ready to strike, but I ignored His warning. I called Abel into the field and slew him and watched as his blood seeped into the soil I had planted.

Why did I do it? God rejected my sacrifice and accepted Abel's and I became jealous. Were the fruits of my harvest not good enough compared with Abel's best flocks? It was not I who rejected God — I was rejected by Him. I felt spurned and anger overtook me, so I left my mark on this world. I went out into the fields and slew my brother.

I was the first to do this.

I would not be the last.

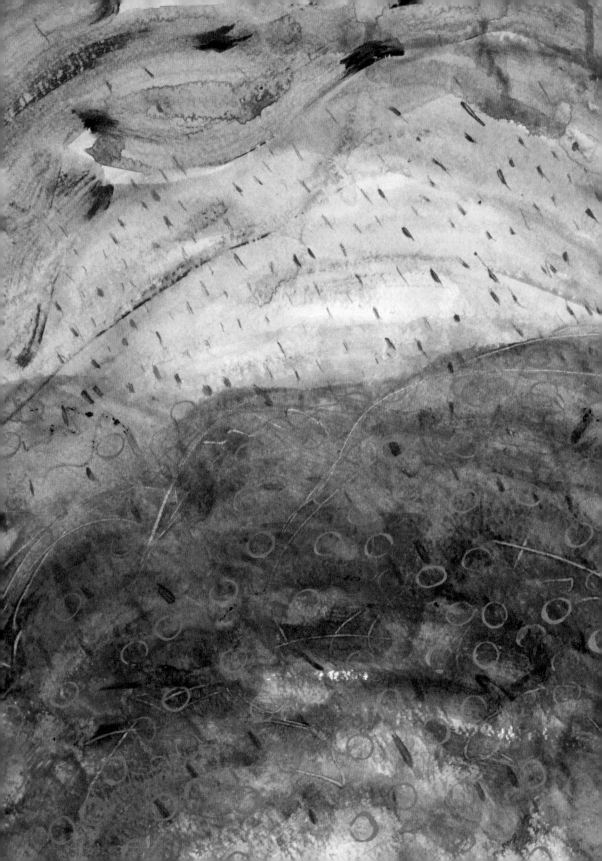

NOAH'S WIFE

The story does not name me, but I shared the burdens of my husband's task. Was I any less righteous and good-hearted than Noah? Did I not walk blameless alongside him? Neither dove nor raven can deny my presence.

It rained for forty days and nights, and the water surged over the earth, and the winds blew us first in one direction and then in another for one hundred and fifty more days. It would be another hundred and fifty days before the water diminished enough for us to finally feel dry land beneath our feet. That's a long time to be cooped up in a leaky boat with all those animals.

And not one of each animal – not two of each, as some people say – but seven pairs of each of the clean ones and one pair of the unclean ones. They were all unclean, if you ask me, doing their animal business everywhere. And who do you think had to clean it all up?

Do you think Noah would have helped? "I'm tired," he would say. "It was hard work building this ark and my old bones are sore. After all, I'm 600 years old." Well, he wasn't too tired to plant a vineyard when the waters finally receded or too old to get drunk on his homemade wine. Surrounded by all that water, his lips thirsted for something I could not offer. We do not speak of the details of that drunken night.

And through it all, I labored on, doing the hard work and never complaining. There's hardly a word in the story about me – not even my name – but I was right there beside him, floating all the way across the water in that rickety boat that smelled of tar and pitch and the waste of a thousand creatures. I cleaned up after those animals, watched the signs and shared the journey with him as we replanted and our sons repopulated the earth. At night I think of all that was lost forever in those dark waters; the memories come flooding back to me in a torrent of tears.

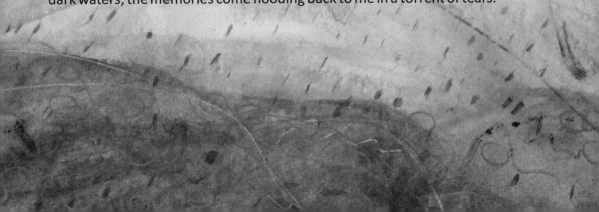

LOT'S DAUGHTERS

The truth is – after all of that fire and brimstone, and then watching our own mother turn into a pile of salt before our very eyes, we thought it was just the three of us left in the world. And since we had found all that wine in the cave, it seemed like the whole thing was ordained by God. How else could just the three of us repopulate the world?

So, yes, we got our father drunk and...well, you know the sorry story. We each had a son from that union, and from those sons came kings and prophets.

I guess we really never had what you'd call a great upbringing, living in Sodom. The memory of that time is like salt in a very fresh wound. We were deserted and alone in a city that was well watered with greed and evil.

And don't get us started on how our father tried to offer us to all those men who were trying to have their way with God's messengers just before all the destruction began. "Here are my two daughters," our father said. "They have known no man. Let me bring them out unto you and do to them whatever you will."

Is this a thing a normal father would say?

So don't judge us for getting him drunk in the cave and having our way with him.

God did tell Abraham he'd spare the city if he could find ten good souls in Sodom, but they were not to be found.

We were the best of the lot.

We were the ones he saved.

HAGAR

To understand my story, you must read between the lines. Listen to what is *not* said as much as what is told. Abraham received great wealth as a result of his deceptions in Egypt. He came away with sheep and cattle, donkeys and slaves. But falsehoods have a way of snaking back around and biting you.

I am Hagar, the Egyptian slave girl, handmaiden to Sarah. My son is Ishmael, who would one day become the patriarch of an entire nation. Sarah had given me to Abraham as a wife because she was unable to bear him children, then drove me away with the boy when he was thirteen.

Ishmael's descendants will reappear soon enough to play a role in this unfolding story, for God weaves His web like no other master. You think He is not a trickster? When Ishmael was grown, God opened Sarah's womb so that she could have a child of her own.

And where did that leave us?

Sarah treated me harshly and demanded that her husband expel us, perhaps fearful that the boy would lay claim to Abraham's holdings as the first-born son —or worse, harm her child.

It was an evil thing to demand, Abraham argued. Not very sporting. Abraham, of course, refused at first – for he truly loved the boy and enjoyed the comforts of my tent.

God prevailed upon Abraham to listen to Sarah – promising him that an entire nation would spring from his loins – and we were sent away with nothing but a skin of water and some bread. We wandered into Beersheba, a dry and dusty place, and when our water ran dry, I surrendered. I placed my son under a tree and wept, certain that we would perish. But fortune's well can often be found lying at your feet. God heard our cry and an angel opened my eyes to the water that was nearby. We drank and survived.

God would soon have an even harsher test in store for Abraham to endure.

ISAAC UNBOUND BY ABRAHAM

Perhaps you have noticed I do not say much. I'm what you'd call the middle man; son of Abraham, father of Jacob and Esau. Father led me up the mountain for three days, only to strap me down to an altar he built. He took out his long knife, ready to slay me right then and there — and he would have too, if it hadn't been for a messenger of God who stopped him at the last minute.

What was that all about, anyway? If I ever admitted to hearing voices in my head telling me to slay my son, they'd have me locked up in a Canaanite minute. Probably throw away the key, too. How old was Father then — one hundred? A man is likely to hear voices in his head when he's that old. There's a name for that, though, hearing voices in your head.

What exactly was the point of that whole sacrifice thing? To show how devoted to God my father was? To show that Father was willing to sacrifice the thing he loved most in the world? What kind of screwy test was that? Honestly, I don't give a ram's horn about the lesson it teaches.

Back then, they said Father talked directly to God and God answered him. Father sure argued with God about sparing the people of Sodom. Did he care for the people who dwelled in the Cities of the Plain more than he did for me? Nothing is said of what we spoke about after that day. We went up to Mount Moriah together; father returned with his servants. I did not follow.

Mother died shortly after he got back. Perhaps this was one test she could not endure.

Later, Father would take another wife who would bear him more children. He was always being pulled in different directions...and torn up inside by the claims everyone was making on his heart. I know he never made peace with sending Hagar and Ishmael out into the desert with only bread and a skin of water. He followed Sarah's wish and banished them both, but we always knew where to find them; when Father died, it was Ishmael and I who went together to bury him in the caves at Machpelah. Ishmael may have been cast out, but he was never far from home — or far from our father's heart.

ESAU'S TALE

Okay, so I sold my birthright for a bowl of red lentils. I admit it was an impulsive thing to do, and I am an impulsive and hotheaded man; nothing like my twin brother, Jacob, the mild-mannered one. I can see how some people might think that selling something like that is disrespectful – as if I despised my own birthright. But how does Jacob emerge as the good son in this story?

I wasn't the one who took advantage of my brother's hunger so I could claim his birthright. Wouldn't a decent brother just offer a bowl of pottage? And I wasn't the one who lied and tricked my half-blind father into believing I was the other son, stealing the blessing for the firstborn, too. That blessing was a big deal back then. Later, when the old man realized what he'd done, he trembled.

When I look back on it, Jacob was always after me. Even as we entered the world together, his hand was grabbing my heel. Well, you can't go around doing that kind of stuff your whole life and not have it come back and kick you in the pants. One day his own sons will lie to *him* and break *his* heart.

When I heard he had stolen my blessing, I was truly angry. I hated Jacob and wanted to slay him for fooling our father and getting the blessing that was meant for me. You can say it was our mother's idea, but Jacob went along with her plan. He never questioned it – except to say he was afraid our father would discover the treachery and he'd be cursed by the old man instead of blessed.

My mother lost me that day too with her trickery. She said she was following God's will to have her older son serve the younger one, but I never served Jacob. Did she have no faith that God's will would prevail without her intervention? She had to go and take matters into her own hands – and look what travails that yielded.

Or was it something else? Did our father really know all along that those arms wrapped in goat skins were not mine? Did he and our mother sit up one night and devise a plan for Jacob to flee to Haran and meet Laban's daughters? It would not surprise me. That kind of deceit is as abundant as the dew. My parents wanted Jacob to marry in the family – and were already upset with me for taking two Hittite wives; perhaps they plotted together to get Jacob to flee. Surely he could tell the difference between his sons. "The hands are the hands of Esau, but the voice is the voice of Jacob," he said, making Jacob sweat with fear.

I was so angry about the whole thing that I wondered how I could get back at them all. I went and looked up Ishmael – my father's half-brother. Ishmael was Abraham's *other* son, the firstborn one he had with Hagar, the servant woman. That side of the family sure understood what it was like to be cast off and discarded. I married one of Ishmael's daughters, and you should have seen the look on Isaac's face when I introduced them to each other. He could sure see *her* plain enough!

Over time, my anger cooled and my fortunes multiplied along with my offspring. When Jacob finally came back home, I met him on the field, surrounded by four hundred of my best men. I could have squashed him like a bug – but instead, I embraced him. I gave him a big hug and a kiss on the neck. Some people said I really wanted to bite him on the neck – but it's not true; time and my own good fortune had long healed all my wounds.

Coming to meet him with four hundred men on the field might have given Jacob the impression I would smite him and his entire family. But I only wanted to put a little fear into his soul. He was so scared of what would happen that he prayed to God that night... wrestled with that angel on the banks of the Jabbok all night long and maybe looked deep into his own heart for the first time. He had his name changed from Jacob to Israel that night. He was hobbled now, but no longer Jacob, the crooked one.

God is often revealed when you least expect it, sending messengers for us to learn from. Everyone has a role to play – though we may not realize it at the time. I guess you could say I moved Jacob closer toward a better path in life. We were twin brothers after all. Were we so different?

LABAN

They make a big deal of me noticing the ring and bracelets that Abraham's servant gave my sister at the well that first day, as if I were only concerned with material goods. What's the big deal? Don't make more of the story than there is.

I admit I am a shrewd man and I wanted to make sure our family stayed together. When Abraham's servant came to get a wife for his son Isaac – you know that poor boy the old man almost sacrificed up on the mountaintop – my mother asked me to negotiate the deal and so naturally I did most of the talking. But the decision about marrying the boy was Rebecca's.

Then, years later when Isaac's son Jacob came to me seeking refuge after fleeing the family because of some big feud, I provided it. He was family. I gave him a job, for heaven's sake. And a wife. Two wives, in fact. And handmaidens, too. He had his way with all of them, that boy did.

When he came to me, he was just a boy on the run, and when he left, he had eleven strapping sons and a daughter and grandchildren too numerous for an old man to count. But what a twisted family that was! I should have known as soon as I heard about the old man wanting to take a meat cleaver to his son. Then *that* boy's son came to me, afraid for his life, spinning a tale about how his brother wanted to kill him for stealing a birthright and a blessing. That is some family we let my sister marry into.

It was the boy, Jacob, who set the bride price, and I thought the offer was fair: work for seven years and he could have my daughter's hand in marriage. After all, he came with nothing, not even money for a dowry. Was it my fault that the boy was rash and impetuous? He was supposed to be the calm, calculating one. Shouldn't he have known it was our custom to always marry the eldest daughter first? Well, he never showed much respect for the firstborn, did he?

He got my oldest daughter's hand in marriage and then worked another seven years for my other daughter. But I paid in advance. I let him take Rachel just a week after he took Leah for a bride, so it wasn't like I made him work another seven years before he could have her. He had them both. I know this kind of thing is frowned upon now, but in our day it was done all the time. Surely, you've heard of the Levirate marriage? Some of the boys didn't like it, but tradition is important.

Jacob stayed with me and worked for six more years after he worked those first fourteen years for my girls. I paid him handsomely with some of my best flocks.

I admit I tricked him into marrying Leah first, but didn't the boy trick his own father in a similar way? Didn't his own father call him Esau and he answered to that name? Poetic justice, we called it when we switched brides – and had a good belly laugh at the time. Even Jacob saw the irony and laughed with us. You think it was a coincidence that the trickster ended up being tricked? Then you don't know whose hand is moving all the pieces around on the board. Yes, Jacob served me – but he served a greater role as well. Did not the children of those unions produce a nation, just as their God had foretold?

When Jacob finally decided to go home – and to take my two daughters and the two handmaidens I gave them, and all my grandchildren and all his spotted flocks with him – the boy just took off like a thief in the middle of the night, while I was off shearing sheep. He didn't even tell me he was leaving after all those years together. What kind of man acts like that? Did he really think I would harm him? Ah, the party I would have thrown for them if I had only known! I would have serenaded them with songs on the harp, but no, he just pulls out without even a goodbye.

When I caught up with them, I asked, "Why did you carry away my daughters and my grandchildren and did not tell me that I might have kissed them all goodbye? Are these not my children?" I could have done him much harm, but his God was watching and had warned me to let him be. I made a covenant with Jacob that day and I kept my word to him. I kissed my daughters and my grandchildren. I blessed them and I departed.

ZILPAH AND BILHAH

We were the lesser wives of Jacob: politely called "handmaidens," because "slaves" is too harsh a word. We are the matriarchs whose names you have to look up.

Jacob always played favorites, and so does the story. His favoritism led to much heartache for all of us.

The story mostly talks about Leah and Rachel, whom we served. But we also lay with Jacob and gave him sons. We did not need spirits or mandrake roots to perform our tricks and wonders.

Are we not also mothers?

From our wombs have come tribes as well, yet there is but a brief mention of our names, only to tell which boys we birthed, nursed, and nurtured into adulthood.

Those were often bitter years. We were given to Rachel and Leah by Laban as wedding gifts to serve them. And later, when they could not bear children, Rachel and Leah gave us to Jacob to serve him in more fundamental ways, so that their houses could be built up through us.

And build we did. We bore him sons: Dan, Naphtali, Gad, Asher. We were nothing more than the fields Jacob planted with his seed.

But did bearing him sons stop the bickering and dissension in the tents? Not at all.

Jacob loved us even less than he loved Leah. When he feared his brother would smite him on the fields near Penuel, he placed us and our children on the field out in front, with Leah and her children behind us, and then finally Rachel and Joseph. He was not about to sacrifice his favorites first, as his grandfather was prepared to do.

Not Jacob.

It is no secret that Jacob loved Rachel more than Leah. In fact, Leah never found favor in his eyes, perhaps because each time he looked at her he saw weakness. Perhaps he saw his own weakness, a reminder of his own treachery and deceit. It was the last of that old trick, haunting him once more.

Treachery and lies beget only more treachery and lies. We weren't the ones who stole Laban's idols and hid them in our saddlebags and we weren't the ones who lied to the old man when he came searching for them, spinning a tale that we could not get off our cushions because the ways of a woman were upon us.

"With whomever you find your gods, that person shall not live," Jacob told Laban, not knowing that it was Rachel who had taken them and had them hidden still. Jacob cursed his true love then, though he did not know it.

The idols were not found by Laban or Jacob or by anyone else, but Rachel, indeed, did not live much longer: she died as her last issue came into the world. Benjamin, the son of Jacob's old age, was born, and Jacob's heart cried again in silence as he buried Rachel by the road to Ephrath.

But who will stop to mark *our* graves with stones?

Where do *our* bodies lie?

DINAH

I am not to be judged. My story is filled with strife and shame – not for what was done to me, but because of what happened afterward: that dirty business down in Shechem when my brothers Simeon and Levi took revenge on the whole town after I had been abused.

That boy – the son of Hamor, the Hivite prince – saw me out in the fields and took me and lay with me and humbled me. Royalty often feels they have the power to take what they want by force, but he loved me and his words spoke to my heart. He said he wanted to marry me and have me as his wife, but my brothers were incensed. I admit, asking for my hand in marriage after he had had his way with me was putting the cart before the donkey, but tell me, that never happened before?

When the Prince's son came with his father and asked for my hand in marriage, my brothers deceived them. They asked that every man in Shechem be circumcised, and Hamor and his son readily agreed. Hamor came right to the gate of the town and spoke to his people, and they ceded to my brothers' request, knowing they would benefit if our nations merged.

When they were all in their tents, nursing their wounds, my brothers Simeon and Levi took their swords and entered the city, killing every single male as they lay there. Prince Hamor. His son. Everyone. There were no guards watching the city because they were all recuperating. My brothers ransacked the town. They took all the cattle, sheep, donkeys, and dry goods. They took the children and women captive. They looted all the houses and said it was punishment for my defilement.

It was not Israel's proudest moment.

Indeed, my father had little to say about any of this, worried only about what other nations would do about this deceit; afraid that the family would now be attacked. On his deathbed years later, he scolded Simeon and Levi for their actions, reminding them that he never forgot their evil deeds. He wouldn't bless them or give them a land holding. After all those years. I took some satisfaction in that.

But not once did anyone ask me what I wanted. Not once was I allowed to speak. My story begins and ends there.

JOSEPH'S BROTHERS

Yes, we threw him in the pit. And yes, we let the Medianite merchants pull him out and sell him to the slave traders who took him away to Egypt.

We bloodied up that coat of his so our father would think Joseph was mauled by a wild animal. We used the blood of a goat kid on the cloak – an ironic touch, don't you think? We had all heard the story of how our father used a slaughtered goat kid and a false garment to deceive his own father.

That boy Joseph was a royal pain in the rear. Always showing off that multicolored cloak of his, just to remind us how much more our father loved him than he loved any of us.

And Joseph kept telling us those crazy dreams he had – and what they meant; where the sun and the moon and the stars would bow down to him, and how one day we would all be bowing down to him. A little haughty, don't you think? Full of himself. "Master of dreams," we called him. It was almost as if he was asking to be thrown into a pit. He needed to be taken down a bit and taught a little humility.

But don't you think what we did was all part of the grand plan so the Lord could work His will? How else would we have all ended up in Egypt for four hundred years so we could be redeemed with that mighty hand and that outstretched arm? Remember that promise God made to Abraham? How would it have happened without Joseph coming first as a slave and telling his dreams to the Egyptian Pharaoh, and then storing grain for the coming famine so we'd come around later seeking food to feed our families? We were simply the instruments that helped set this into motion. Even Joseph said as much. "The famine is upon us," he said, "And God has sent me before you to preserve life." Well, we're glad that's how he thinks.

And glad he doesn't hold any grudges. "It is not you who sent me down to Egypt," Joseph told us, "but God. While you meant to do evil toward me, God meant good." Well, we are thankful he has shown compassion and forgiven us. There's a lesson there.

JOSEPH

It is no accident that the story says we descended into Egypt. There is no subtlety there. Descend we did, lowering ourselves pretty deep into our own pit. I have many regrets now, thinking back.

I served God, but I also served Pharaoh, and that was a devil's bargain for sure. I taxed the Egyptians to please Pharaoh, even though I knew it was God Himself who saved me from the dungeon and death. I changed my dress and allowed Pharaoh to change my name and give me a wife from his people. Not just any woman – but the daughter of an Egyptian priest.

As Pharaoh's agent, I collected food for seven years and piled up stores like the grains of sand in the sea. I counted grain until I could count no more. When famine came, I sold the grain I had stored. I gathered all the money and silver I had collected and brought it to Pharaoh. With no money, the Egyptians were desperate and eager to sell their livestock. We took their horses, cattle, and donkeys and gave them bread and they were happy. The next year they had neither money nor livestock. The people begged me to take their land in exchange for bread, which I did.

In this way, the Egyptians became subjected to Pharaoh's will, and I was their shepherd, driving them to him. I gained possession of all the land for Pharaoh and removed the people from their homes, town by town – from one Egyptian border to the other. It was a shrewd move to sever the people from their own land and place them on lands they had no connection to. I gave the Egyptian people the seed to sow the land and took one-fifth of their crops for Pharaoh. I saved their lives in the famine, and they were grateful. In exchange, they gave up everything.

My family joined me in Egypt and increased in numbers into a great and prosperous nation, just as it had been written. In time, this bred resentment among the Egyptians. When a new Pharaoh arose who did not know me or any of my generation, he saw only the wealth and power of my descendants and enslaved them all, fearful they would become a threat.

They tell my story as if I was a masterful administrator to a king. But when I look back, I see only a well of regret.

JACOB

Did I get what I wanted? Did I get all I sought?

I took the birthright and the blessing from my own brother Esau but I paid a heavy price for it, living in fear of him for all those years; forced to flee my home and live like a stranger in a strange land with my guilt buried deep inside.

I wanted Rachel as a wife, but had to work long and hard for her, putting up with the enmity and competition between Rachel and her sister that turned our lives as bitter and empty as a barren womb.

I was blessed with twelve sons and a daughter, but two of those boys were real hotheads, quick to anger, seeking revenge when calm and thoughtfulness was what was needed. Another crossed a line that I will not even discuss. There was always ill will among my children … perhaps because I was never able to treat them all the same.

I have lived a long and fruitful life. Perhaps not as long as my father and grandfather, but a life that has clearly left a mark on the generations.

Was it a good life? Yes, surely it was, but I had more than my share of sadness and pain. I grieved for my favorite son for years, only to find him alive again in the end.

I will carry my grief over Rachel's death with me forever.

I was rich. I was successful. But was I really happy with the way things turned out?

I cannot answer that question. It is something I still wrestle with.

Other Books by Barry Louis Polisar

Telling The Story: A Passover Haggadah Explained
Stolen Man
Something Fishy
Curious Creatures
Peculiar Zoo
Insect Soup
Dinosaurs I Have Known
Don't Do That: A Child's Guide to Bad Manners
The Haunted House Party
The Trouble With Ben
Noises From Under the Rug
A Little Less Noise
Snakes! And the Boy Who Was Afraid of Them
The Snake Who Was Afraid of People

Visit Barry on the web: www.Barrylou.com

Retelling Genesis
© 2014 by Barry Louis Polisar
All Rights Reserved
ISBN 10 # 0-938663-97-6
ISBN 13 # 978-0-938663-97-3

Illustrations by Roni Polisar
Typography and Design by Christa McInturff

Published by Rainbow Morning Music
2121 Fairland Road
Silver Spring, Maryland 20904